Sakineh Asadzadeh was born in Iran, and did PhD in Private Law. She is working in Ministry of Justice as a law employee (also, she was the law member in specialized commission of legal counsel about the trade affaires). Sakineh was the political assistant in ministry of foreign affairs, research assistant and translator in International Association of University Muslim Professors. She is also a professor of law in the university.

Her awards; "The First International Scientific, Literature and Arts Festival of Sa'di/2020," "Second National Festival of Superior Writes of Human Sciences (Allameh Jafari)/2020,"

"The 4th Festival of the Best Dissertations of Iran (Special Award of Professor Hesabi) /2020," (Superior Researcher/2018), (Best Law Employers/2017).

Poetic life: She started her poetic life when she has 4 years old and then she won a prize by participating in the hymnody group in the highschool. Her poems have been published in several magazines in some countries; such as " Hayat Gölgesı, Zaman Çekırdekcesı (Şıırden Dergısı, 69 sayisi, Turkiye), Regret for the soil (Grihaswamini, international e-magazine,2021, India), Distillate of Bittern and Solar of Buttercups (Atunis Galaxy Poetry, 2021, Netherland), Göklerın Yüzü (Şıırden Dergısı, 60 sayisi, Turkiye), Benim Ağır Kederım (Şıırden Dergısı, 59 sayisi, Turkiye), Hayalin Dansi and Aşkın Tekbırı (Şıırden Dergısı, 58 sayisi, Turkiye), Dileğın Tonu (Şıır Sarnıcı, n° 13, 2022, Turkiye), La fuga del venerdi (La casa della poesie di como, 2022, Italy), Kozadan Kaçan Kelebekler/Zaman Mecunu/Sadece Sen Bana Anlam Ver (Şıırden Dergısı, 74 sayisi, Turkiye),

زاغک پریشان (روزنامه سراسری سایه ,شماره 2257 ,ایران)، گزاره های قصر (مجله اطلاعات هفتگی ,شماره 3962 ,ایران)، گوشواره عقیق (انجمن علمی مطالعات صلح ایران ,یادداشت صلح شماره 14 ,1400 ,ایران)، قوس و قزح دیدگانت (روزنامه سراسری سایه ,شماره 2547 ,ایران)، آینه جهان بین (روزنامه سراسری سایه ,شماره 2546 ,ایران)، موسم دلدادگی و به تو مجبور است دلم (ماهنامه هنرمندان آریائی ,شماره 3 ,ایران)، به تو مجبور است دلم (روزنامه سراسری سایه ,شماره 2571 ,ایران)، حقیر من اللّسان و إبتسام الحبّ (مجلة دیوان العرب، 1444 ه.ق).

Her poetry books: (*Hayali Damlacik*, Şıırden Yayıncılık, Turkiye, 2019), (*Under the azure sky*, Anthology Bilingual,

India, 2020), (Atunis Galaxy Anthology, Lulu press, South California, 2022) and Persian prints include:

قطره چکان خیالی، 1397، انتشارات نارون دانش. بیدمشک عناب، 1398، انتشارات نارون دانش. لعل خاکستری، 1398، انتشارات نارون دانش. ماه نو، مجموعه شعر، انتشارات نارون دانش، 1399. رعد آتشین، انتشارات ارشدان، 1399. قاصدک پیر، انتشارات آنان، 1401. ته سیگارها پر از اندیشه اند، 1400، انتشارات آنان. به وقت صفر، 1400، انتشارات آنان. سه آ، 1400، انتشارات آنان.

Artistic life: She participated in some international art galleries; such as " Aşk Kadını, 2022, Turkiye", "Kala Vithika, 2022, India ", " Las Laguna, 2022, California". Her paints "Dertli Anahtar" and "Garden of Love" have printed by international art magazine of Parsforte, summer 2022 in Italy (also this magazine has published her biography in spring 2022). Then she published her first art book nominated "Hidden Found "in 2022 in Iran.

Scientific Life: She wrote twelve articles about the contracts and comparative studies of agreements and two law books "Legal Status of Contractual Groups" and "Contract Salvation Rule (With the Comparative Approach in French Law)". Asadzadeh's favorites are playing piano, music, exercise, reading law, literature and culture books.

For my sweetie,

The one and only,

Eternal shine in my life, "My mom"

And…

For, "My dear brother"

The great supporter,

And supplier.

Sakineh Asadzadeh

MUSTARD EARRING

AUSTIN MACAULEY PUBLISHERS™
LONDON • CAMBRIDGE • NEW YORK • SHARJAH

Ordering Information
Quantity sales: Special discounts are available on quantity purchases by corporations, associations, and others. For details, contact the publisher at the address below.

Publisher's Cataloging-in-Publication data
Asadzadeh, Sakineh
Mustard Earring

ISBN 9781685626136 (Paperback)
ISBN 9781685626143 (ePub e-book)

Library of Congress Control Number: 2023900486

www.austinmacauley.com/us

First Published 2023
Austin Macauley Publishers LLC
40 Wall Street, 33rd Floor, Suite 3302
New York, NY 10005
USA

mail-usa@austinmacauley.com
+1 (646) 5125767

Many thanks to my university professors, my poem cooperator, Metin Cengiz and the groups of Siirden Yayincilik.

1. Escape of Fridays

Fly on…
The restless and riotous existence
From the horrors
Trample…
On the earthy restrictions
And rescue your straggler soul
From all of fake taboos
Here… You and me…
Are the voices of together
And endless of sky
Is the fascination in our hearts
Let's dispart
Our sweet feelings
And our world
To be freed…
From the loneliness and big-headed
I am effecter of silence
For your speeches
About the stable and certainty love
To drown into eternity permanence
In humanity…

2. The Isolation of the Resurrection

It seems you decide to let me off every moment
The most way letting off than staring
Staring at the isolation of the resurrection
The most letting off than disappearing
Disappearing at the end of the restriction
You know better than me
I run out of the loneliness

3. Smile of Love

When your eyes smile
The love whispery enters in my heart dorm
And the ambiguity planet of your look
Kisses the end most of my emotion
And the moon…
The moon disappears
Between my conscious and my mind
Between the love to flying
Between me to me

4. Sandy Hours Atelier

Whatever I breathe
I find love
With the colorful smile
Full of ghosts
My soul wants…
Standing up the time
To frame the love
On the assumption of stability
And my fiction wants…
The companion of sandy hours with the moments
For the loss of concupiscence and the sparkle of the
isolation of the pronoun
I'll take you
To the turbulence of life
And I'll be nearby of the ocean of time
Until the end of fusing
You're vault
Beyond the moving
Beyond the feeling

5. Unlimited Reticence

I will see for the last time; impavid
To the pansy's rain squall
To the floodwater of intense cold
In the carpet buyer's marketplace
There is the quotation
The spring has come and
The wind inspects
Autumn that has become victim for the conjecture
Because of absolute loneliness
And the guilt is chosen the reticence
Unlimited reticence
Absit omens the leafs of embarrassment will shed
Absit omens the autumn will repeat again
Oh… My Tehran's roof
I wish a sopor until
When I will open my eyes
I will experience the spring with your eyes
An endless experience

6. The Seasons of Crayon

The autumn comes and me…
Under the crepitation of anguish leafs
My back breaks
What's the beautiful!
These backbreaking
And getting colorful
By the season's crayon
Orange…
Yellow…
Aquamarine…

7. Blowguns

My inside has been filled with deepness of looking at
dingy scarecrows
Between swith of ruinations
In the summit of death the humanity
Oh… Infected conscience by urticarial
I surrender you…
To the airflow's vexillums…
To the memorial of clock's cupolas of joining crossroad
To the heavenly hands of callose and bitter hurricanes
And I swear on the multiplicative seconds of blowguns
On the inauspicious memories of cracking up my one-
hundred-seventy
Rain the affection and life rainsquall
For washing my thought from despicable ancestry
Until the borders of amorousness
For done charming
With boozer nebulas
In the mercy and generosity alleys

8. Earthly Bodies

My mind became aged and senile
Because of flying the twilight tulips
Tonight, without any excuse and reason
I will condemn the moon
To the life imprisonment in oubliette of silences
To the chiliad centuries of quite
Because of crime the requesting of absolute darkness
I will crucify the earthly bodies
I will lock the time
Until killing the self
It seems my land people's crime
Is the most outbalance than eating the apple
Here the looks are for selling
The words also…
Are grandmother's textural hanks
I don't know why
The heroes of epopee are on the death squads yet and
We are searching the story of Hussain Kurd Shabestari

9. Stricken Rocks

I pass by avarice alleys
Towards the impasse imaginations
Imaginations without any splendor
I said hello
For blooms of flagon's penitence
I wash my mind
From the hubris fire
The calycles are laughing frigidity yet
And are turning back on shout and eclipse words
Like downfall of raindrops
On bowl of disquietude and perturbation
Here… it's a magus land
The ladybugs are mourning too
And the rocks will be strike
I conjuncture in the date of despairing
From hoping…
And wishing the hidden locks of my mind
And sometimes I search the luminosity
In hands of thatches
Under oodles misery and pain
It seems the wind's face also has been broken

And the moonlight… shiny mirror of entity

Has been lost its own glitter

Under sclerosis fences of dream

10. Rift of Friday

What's strange

Losing in yourself

And descending on broad territory of expectance

And being comfort for the times

On the earthy hill of time

Being divergent of love what's colorful love

Smelling the rose water

Aromatizing with purity

Be among the barrier between the two aged worlds

The world of compensation and preservation

Today…

I was on the bottom of blaze of jug

And tomorrow I will be on the climax of ascent of amorous

What's attractive

Unlimited qualifications of daybreak's slogan

And became standing on the beloved angle

Oh… The conceptual butterfly…

You have been shone on top of my heart's roof

Be pure and full of novelties for me

Because you are adjudication the records of sunset
And the indicative antecedent of shout
You are infinite banner of merged of place
On grades the rift of popular Fridays

11. I'll Still Want You

I was grown-up en masse
And the pieces of my existence speared on the land
You… wild lotus
And you… locust of Ctesiphon
Much as you dig my own grave
I'll still want you
Like a cold wind…
And a cool and attractive anemone

12. Buds of Sorrow

Every time the sorrow populate
My eyes blooms
And the chagrin sits on my heart's roof
Warble…
And the nerves coils on the torsion of my heart's
arterioles
It seems you and me are the ambiguous word
And full of ferrum conundrum
In shiny configuration of cold
Urticarial with striped odd even checks
Attached on crystal cassock
Oh bloom of cherry
Chant of being with you
Is fiddled the phrases
And is dried the sentences
It seems the juror of love
Finds out the certain that the treatment of heart
Is the crushed

13. Unclean Oreganos

At the night
I woke up
I seeded some scions of oregano
Between the turquoises
Then I closed my eyes
Oreganos and turquoises
After me…
Concluded the fraternity together
To grow for each other
And to wilt for each other
The days elapsed and every one of two lovers
Is became sturdy their roots
But fears of turquoise became lots
Oregano of the story is uncleaned too
The plague of niggardliness and envy
From while they companions with tragacanth's taboo
Tragacanth of egoism and fretfully
The lover… turquoise is demoralized
Unclean oregano to the niggardliness digs every day
On grave of livid turquoise
And the upset turquoise weepy
Talks to himself
Yes… that's it

Slashing by acquainted one
The same pretentious acquainted
The same famous acquainted

14. The Firedrakes of Patch

Oh… Blind malkins
Shelter to me
Because in the season of hunting
The firedrakes is became the life hunter and
The tulips of champaign
Ill and lurid
And the sky's sight is stamped on the bywords pages
And also the rain's eye shines on the dead prairie
With amorous fondled
And sweet odor of flower dances
With oriental chant
And it paints the face of sleeping
In the pure mirrors
Oh …blind malkins know that
The time will be stopped
When the love shines

15. Surges of Laugh

The beach of my heart
Woke up of the sleeping of the people of cave again
It heads on peacock's shoulders
And calls the polar storms always attacks on duns
And the turquoise wings of depth of sea
But at the depth of sea…
The fishes of territory of bamboos seethe continuous When
they behold the sea of adulatory laughs
They aspire at droughty
Into flagon of the evenfall of luminescent
The same evenfall that …
Sky's view is became the unglazed pendulum
Like a simulacrum of the gong of beach lanterns
And lifesaving of surges of laugh rasps the petrous
figures of sea
Onto expectation the lumpy sea of the stars
And looking at the migration of Asperitas clouds
Oh… Calmness of my life
Here, the spirit of polar aurora realizes too

16. Rara Avis of Eden

I am free of chicanery
I am free of colloquium
I am sitting on the reclusive corner
To wait the boom of cloud
And to erupt the patience
In the hidden house of love
Sickly and truculent
I speared the chant of spring
On the aortic inanition
With expectation and chagrin of resemble
I am departing the monastery of straw bloodsuckers
On the torsion of Ctesiphon's gnomons of skyline
I dangle the rainbow balance to the foundation of orrery
attitude
And I replace laugh with aggrieved at the
Broad-mindedness of colorful swallow of twilight
I present the lyres of pain wish to the grace gnostic
facies
For complying the minstrel of myself
Oh … Rara avis of monster that is more immortal than Eden
Be pioneer sunshine on memories of cirrus of Kasraa
That the timpani of bliss is started playing the willingly
aster

17. White Nightmare

I want to wake up
Of this white nightmare
Of this folly sleeping
That is etherized my whole
I want to enter to death chariot
And to head on sluggard sinters bedside
I want to be another aurora
Mounting on collars of order
To close my eyes toward all of life lotteries
I want to incarcerate the beauty in solitude gallery with
myself and my negligences
And to entrust colorful pencil to the designator hand of wind
For painting the unique mind nature
And you… Oh the most wilderness of mirage of life
I can focus on well with you
I can think better with you
I can soar to the head of cuckoo effigies
And I sit on to look at the azure stars
I count the most nebular of inanition imagine
And you… Oh autumn idiotism
Remember the eternal acronical

The same acronical that…
The moonbeam gild the land
And with coming the daybreak
It endows the land to the sun

18. Tremor of Rain

Do you hear the tremor of rain?
That it drizzles on the mirror frame of land
The same tremor… Plays with the storm of pain the
Chute tragedies and descent symphonies
I didn't want more to touch the time
At the dungeons of epochs
I didn't want more to embay the true
At the almshouse of closes
That the ignorance adjudicates
And my heart was archived
At the shrine of the infidel priestess
And the dictums consecutive were dited
On the floorage of aboveboard of arsenal
Oh invitation of luminosity on the grain field of glory
and splendor
Oh the plainsong of ascent verses
I want you without any excuse
When the day down shine and the land open the eyes
The fire temples of horrors roar on the dreams
Oh love…
My unique innocence

Burnish my thoughts
And shine on my moonlight galaxy
Because you are reflexing of my soul
In the hidden mirror of simulations

19. Crabbed Instruments

I discover your look's secret away from the tyrannies
You are my inferior inculpation depending on the enlightenment
Like a scarecrow cinereous
Condemned to darkness apart from crayons
Vowed with unstable sounds
Mounted on the body of blacksmith
Stunning by crabbed instruments
Ready to do chamberlain and protection of dusty archives
In addition urticarial hives
Inflammation the old sore
The older than parting
Raid to the detritus of the world
And my main charge is inflammation of hypothesizes and propagation the rules
Oh… the mobile idea turned to the willing slogan
Your survivor is the chattels of houri and faerie
And my survivor is interesting spun on soil of humanity
And the most romantic prayers

20. The Warp and Woof of Seconds

The tick-tock sound of analogs
And the passing of time…
Across the labyrinths of hard
The balance between the sounds
Sewn up to the subsequent
Engraved with mustard textures
Woven on the green branches
Full of glitter of kindness and generosity
Behind the chapters and seasons of time
Lolled on the warp and woof of seconds
Those all are reminiscent of you
The essence of humanity
Joint to the enclosure of silence
With the advice techniques
Coiled on the thatch earrings
You born in village
You are thinking and motivated man
You make the possibility
And you don't have facilities
You are united with sun and clouds
Even the territory also praises your routes
And the day shines on your satisfied face

You have borrowed time
And your guarantee is your shyness
Your guarantor is the owner of the age
Arise and do not be sad

21. Remembering Your Eyes

Sunset…
What a beautiful shade!
On the immaculate face of your millennium horizon
I remember your eyes…
Also the raindrops
I've sworn to prostrate
On the top of dews of your eyelashes
Every time I play the piano
It seems my soul gets elder too and…
My dreams became the real
Beyond the truth…

22. Bobtailed Silence

I'll see you the last time
Impavid to the raining of violets
To flood of intense colds
In the marketplace of carpet salesman
There is a quotation
The spring has come and
The wind inspects the fall
The fall is victim for the suspicion
Because of absolute loneliness
And the guilt is silent
Bobtailed silence
Lest the fronds of embarrassment sheds
Lest the fall repeats again
Oh… the roof of Tehran
I want a heavy sleep
So that when I open my eyes
I can experience spring in your eyes
An endless experience…

23. Saturn of Stupidity

The road devours me
The distresses devours me
And I…
Except of the pieces…
Do not remain in these porches!
My heart is a friary
And my mind has motion
But my eyes have been stained by the blood
The world questions about the dogmatic unknowns
And I left behind of the great known
I am searching the answer
From the drunken narcissus
In the waiting for the conversant guise
I am not aware
I owe a long time breath of life
To that same bibulous
To that same judge of sun
My qualification is clear
Apparently human…but
My heart is boiling of that baseborn Saturn of stupidity
Lower than quiet conscience
Lower than smeary of the soul

24. Colors of Warnings

How can I say goodbye to your eyes, the remnant dew of
the yoke?
In the early of ebbing the awakening of moon
And clouds behind the curtains of silence
While the waiting for hearing the familiar sound
While watching the eclipse of your emotions
Those camp on the eve of the bank of my hands
That they are calling pleadingly your sandy steps
And the water drops are fondling the rockies of your
pain
And I sit strangely and calmly
To wait for the horror of death
To experience the transferring of my earthly soul
To the boundless of infinity

25. Waves of Laughter

The shore of my heart wakes up again from the sleep of the
cave
And rests on the shoulders of the peacock
And it calls the polar storms that are constantly attacking on
the beach sands
And on the turquoise wings of the bottom of the sea
And but …in the bottom of the sea
The fishes of the region of bamboos
Constantly turbulence off
By seeing the raging sea of laughter
And they have whimsy for water
At the dusk glow of the sunset…
The same sunset that the look of sky will became the
pendulum without glaze
The iconographer of bell of lighthouse of beach
And the lifeguard of waves of laughter abrades the rocky
bodies of sea
In the hopping of turbulent sea of stars
And watching the emigration of asperatus priester
Yes, oh… the calm of my life…
Here the spirit of the aurora borealis is also
releasing…

26. The Dagger of the Sun

I will rise again

This time, not for you…

For the fragmentation of my existence

I will roam all the alleys of evil to find the remnants of anger

And I will extinguish my heat, the same constant heat of love

Love for you and your immortality,

Here… the dream is regret

And the sun is dagger on heat bosoms bed

And the night is a short desire stacked of the harvest of moon

And the stars, a delegation of the neglects, sings the verses of love

In the rural retreats of the world

Before the gates of the possibility

And I am still longing for pure recessional

Impregnated with the fancy of actually

I sing about the big subtractions

And I pass among the accumulation of judgments

To reach the waves of turbulence

And I will write you as the beginning and the end of the experience of love

And I will travel to the land of forgetfulness to join the
history of eternity
And more silently than any time
I will whisper to ear of time
Your amorous

27. Autumn Oak

There is no other way
To being like spring
To became colorful
Last night was before sleep awake than ever
And my eyes were more distracted than my heart
As if the rainbow of thoughts didn't fill up the cage… And
chained to revolting of thought
The thought of renewal passes
And lighting the saddler of purity
Pass from the end of inversions
And purity of last romance
I have no expectation about consciousness
I just have expectation about dawning
The gloaming will be shine, the sun will be claw
And aurora will say hello to the bounds
And asleep will threw up the dream into the water
To come for welcome to autumn oak
In the trails of stars party
Brighter than Hoor and Perry
Closer to spring

They fill their piggy bank of senses
From redness and sweetness
And from the chanting of renewal

28. Baptism of Conscience

I will see up your grave clothes like snow
I will bathe you with the water of the river of love
I will pour a sip of you on my memories
And I will entrust you in the hands of the earth
I will chase you away with the cries of my heart
Do not worry…
Your remembrance engraved on the walls of room
Whenever I want, I will squeak you
And your soul will remain in my bag of sincerity

29. The Trembling of the Rain

Do you hear the trembling of the rain?
Which falls on the glass frame of the earth scrappy!
The trembling that plays with the sad storm
Tragedies of downfall…
And Symphonies of descension…
I do not want to touch the time in the black holes of time
I do not want to lock the truth in the poorhouse of the
closings
The ignorance ruled and my hear became archived
At the temple priests irreligious and the dictums
consecutively were dictated
On the open session armories
Oh… The calling of blaze on the grain field of splendor
Oh…The plainsong of ascent verses
I want you without excuse
When the morning shines
And the earth opens eyes and Temples of fear
They shine on dreams
Oh… love
My only innocence
Varnish my thoughts and shine on the moonlight of my

ultra-mundane

Which you are the reflection of my soul

In the hidden mirror of similarities

30. White Nightmare

I want to wake up
From this white nightmare
From this idiot dream that makes etherized my whole
body
I want to step on the chariot of death and disregard for the
dream
I want to head on bedside ashes apathetic
I want to be aurora again
Riding on the collars command
I want to close my eyes on all lots of life
I want to lock beauty in the solitary gallery
With myself and my shortcomings
And I want to entrust the colored pen
In the inscribed hands of wind to draw the most unique
nature of the mind
And you, the most desert mirage of life
You make me precisionist
You make me thoughtful
I can soar on the height of the cuckoo statues and sit
Down to watch the azure stars
And count the most nebular of imaginative rigor
And you…the foolishness autumn
Remember the primordial evening

The same evening that the moonshine was gilt the
ground
And with the coming of dawn
It will deposit the earth to the sun

31. Butterflies Escaping From the Cocoon

Look at the cloudy sky
Waiting for me and you
Clenching our hands and
Embracing the rain
O unique without repetition…
O steady flowers…
Look at the anemones
To the wild spear-grass…
And butterflies escaping from the cocoon
I wish say
If the time stops
And you…
If you look into the darkness of my eyes
If you fall on the horizon of my heart
And hastily whispering
If you meet love
With a bag full of gray stars
And in red, blue and purple colors

32. Just You Give Me Meaning

Just you
Give me meaning
that I am a word
Vast and boundless
you will not find me in no dictionary
Solve me
that I am a mystery
Vague and luxurious
Insoluble and complex
that only you have understood me
Only you know me well…
give me meaning
to smell of petunia flowers, my ashes
and the soil of my grave
After flying
from this land
to be fragrant
In eternal memorial of a romantic whisper
Word by word of indication of my existence
Just you give me meaning

33. Infected Thymes

In the night
I wake up
And I planted some thymes
Among the turquoise flowers
Then I closed my eyes
The thymes and turquoises
After me
Engaged in the fraternization
Growing for each other
And withering for each other
The days passed and both of lovers
Their roots have been strengthened
But the fears of turquoise have been more
The thyme of our story is infected
In the pest of stinginess and jealousy
Every day it cooks the livid turquoise's goose
And the painful thymes weepy
Say to itself
Yes! It is
Received the wound from acquaintance
The same full claim acquaintance
The same well-known acquaintance

34. Messenger of Blame

What unstable time is

Crawls inside occasional seconds

Spears on the unframed rose-water bottle

It's time to announce the ennui

On the atonic encasements of reincarnation

What a strange, time dies me…

Every moment I step

On the soil of joining

One piece of me links with the heartbeat of the earth

My shadow tramples

From being without me, living

I… fearlessly perfumes to the endless smell of winter

The season of coldness

And messenger of blames

What a delicious for me

The story of flags of miscue

O irreverent of darkness

How much is the love?

That the highest elegance is for me

And king of luminosity

At that time it says

The love is like a logic

Without any reason

It is a strange tone
Shakes harvest of the heart
From me and me and me
More effective
Understanding the hidden of life
Which from its harmony is wanting
And how mornings of eastern blooming

35. Zherbera of Bertrand

Again doubts and misgivings
Move with browbeating attitude of
The crucifixion of tsar of the hearts
The knights of czar of gravities
A little bit the seconds stops
For respecting to Zherbera of Bertrand
And the differences became the similarity
To join the two endless galaxies
Sophia and great Fabier
The two embarrassed galaxies but happy
Far away from embers and turbulence
In depth of prays
And romantics
And other side is the separate world
Barren and rebellious
Onto ambush of Zherbera
Turns around this two galaxies
His name is Rafael
His qualities is orrery sun
Burning and shining
And his solemnity is whine and wickedness
Full of regret and aggressive
He didn't know

Love is vicissitude not otherness
This is the same similar different
For Sophia and Fabier
Steps parallel with the doubts
And hugs the unsolved facts like a tun
On the eloquence and rhetoric of speeches
And I… Zherbera of Bertrand
Homogenous with goniometer of love
I always know
The world has a mystery
Carved on recuperation of cruelty
And accepting of courage…

36. Wanted Valley

Oh my wanted valley
What should I look at?
Because you and the meaning of your immortality
Are the whole of my world
Oh the desire and desirable
My whole word
Stand in my two throne eyes
The eternal kindness
What should I think about?
To tranquil my heart
From attachment to your adytum pillars
Oh my companion
And the predecessor marvel without any distinction
Tell me…
What should my eternal patience to do?

37. Queen of Shadow

At sunset
Dawn scattered across the sky
The weather vane is blooming
And a sparrow-like traveler
Curling until morning
Accompany the queen of shadow
With hours of eye contact
Like the ice melted
Or like fire flamed
As if a calm will arise
In the storm of life

38. Shadows of Your Eyes

In this land
When I am walking
I see the effects of love
And foot prints of life
I know, a little further
I will find
The shadows of your eyes
The blues of world's wide vesting
That didn't have any slashing
That didn't have any final
I will share my beauties
With the world creations
I will reflect
The peace of mind and mental
To all of nature
I will remind
The shadows of your eyes
On excuse of my love
My love to see your shiny
My love to feel my heartbeats
Deeply and…
Stable…
Like the power of moon